AFTER

THEM

Jimi McDonnell

Published in 2022 by After Books

Email: jimihair@gmail.com

Cover image: Jimi McDonnell

Cover design: Seán Breathnach

Author photo : Harry Newman

To Saoirse, Issa, Martin, Nicola, Mogs Noelie & Jill

Contents

Promenade

The shape of the Prom was changed
by wizard hats with dull names
and this month is too cold for cones,
so let's join the footfall again.

I can imagine this place renewed
with cars whose tunes shake speakers,
a Morse code for the seekers
propelled by two feet and two wheels.

But traffic's a transient thing -
metal and heat, muscle and meat,
a game that ends in defeat –
when we kick Blackrock's wall.

In this place of movement and speech
the elusive remains out of reach,
asking to stay where it is,
in salted air, in breath, discarded.

Rosses Point

The sea surrounding Rosses Point was clear;
It's crystalline to me as I sit here.
Sligo sang the newness of your touch –
Strange solos soared, and were never long enough.
Did Pearl Jam sound better, or was that me?
Vedder's voice roared, but the bass played softly.
Love, what I hear now is too much birdsong,
An avian chant where the words are wrong.

Of course, it sounds amazing too – I won't be
Getting maudlin, nor lament the spring.
We met last autumn, summer is a new thing
For us, as this, gathering momentum
Like a folk song, a new one for Eddie
Who taught me to sing – when I was ready.

Hometown Sonnet

To check the news ten times a day is cracked.
Numbers change, economies fall. All
That is left is the joy of looking back
At how we dressed for that bleak ball.

Whose hand did you hold as the dying died?
Did some love bring you together?
Or were digits clasped by a new false bride –
Bones knows the lie of forever.

Leave that phone at home, simply turn it off.
Laugh at the jokes you've heard before,
Don't think about the glance or the cough,
Sent to usher you off the floor.

"Well, I never knew" you'll say you said,
About a septic tank, and a thousand dead.

Lenaboy Blues

For Philip & Anna

Let me evoke it
Let me remember
  what I choose to

Our effusive friendship
In the quietude
Where what I could say
  was too finite

Let me listen
To your treatise
  on the stars
Why they have those names
Where the space station is now

And today, especially,
Let me listen
While we sit with Anna
  in your kitchen

As you explain
5/4 time
And that I *can* grasp it
In fact – that I have sung it

Let me think
  here
Let me say
  that you both
  taught me how to grieve

but with that
I have learned
  to live with the limitless
  to pursue words
  to sharpen what I have
  and to drive in silence
  along the Curraghline

No Compass

A garrison town, they call it
But how could this place
ever stoop to the colonial?

Such a thing to have thought
on the way to her house.

You know, the way love corrupts
is the sweetest deceit.
The lies told to our very own cynic,
the half truths we drop on doubt,
like a tincture made from lavender and lemon balm.
We drink it, and we're new.

I could have walked up that hill,
backwards,
on Cuban heels,
and believed an escalator took me there.

Negatively Shop Street

for Aido

You say the words 'banana bread'
Like it's a revolution
Check your tongue, your verbs are wrong
Man, you need elocution!
Where is the Maldron Sea Salt?
Where is the wholemeal flour?
The whole world's going gluten free
And getting thicker by the hour.

I say the phrase 'the printed word'
Like it's some kind of mantra
The Times looks like a trophy
When I'm strutting out of Centra
My t-shirt came from Penney's
But my runners are free trade
I'm moving like De Niro
In the one where he got made!

She woke up in Loughrea,

Threw her hand across my chest

I just read a novel

And forgot about the rest

Her words were an inferno

Our cadence was our own

But my dreams were sleeping elsewhere

I awoke from them alone.

We say the word community

We like to say 'collective'

No one's looking for your bio, mate,

Or a fucking retrospective!

He got published one time,

And he never let it go

His clothes would speak of London

But his eyes just saw Furbo.

They're gunning for the hipsters

They're gunning for St Nic's

They're carving up our city

Those free market pricks!

So put a roof on Shop Street

Call it a shopping mall

The planner took a pill once

But he's not your fucking pal.

The sign that says 'atone, atone'

Is written on a crooked line

Cos the goddess and the guru, both,

Know well how to recline

So live your life to meditate

(Or) give it up to mediation

The words we use and learn to love

Just break our concentration.

No Music Please!

Preheat your oven
To one-eighty degrees
Cook your food well
But no music, please.

Drink irresponsibly
Til half-eleven at least,
Gather outdoors
But no music, please.

Get stuck in traffic
Stock up the jeep
With cheap shit and plastic
But no music, please.

Cat call a woman?
They'll leave you in peace -
Open season for primates
But no music, please.

Meet friends? Absolutely!

You're on day release

But no laughing and dancing –

And no music, please.

Support a musician

Email your TD

Discord sounds amazing

But no music?! *Please!*

From A Dream

You are older now
and I am older still,
but our love is now,
as it was then,
a pure and godly thrill.

If in the confines of the mind,
it seems, we only go uphill,
in the wildlands of the heart,
my love, we roam,
and yet, are still.

So let us say upon this rock
 - our home –
that hurtles round a burning sun
that love is love, and that is all,
and stand together

one.

Someone

Someone, my love, has walked here before us
And I cannot name all the trees.
I keep singing that War on Drugs chorus,
You say 'Jimi, that's enough, please.'

We drive on past Cong to Ardnageeha,
And our feet sound this autumn's crunch –
One whole year of loving you, a
Birthday for us in the Mayo sun.

All the writer's that have gone before me
Have with great eloquence said
That passion's the liquid for dreaming
The brew for the blood in your head.

But that headiness is no everyday thing,
and it's not always needed here.
Silence took us beyond a fling,
To plant ourselves in our own lithosphere.

We break the crust on this new ground,

Impressions heavy with intent

And we won't leave this world as what we found

We will change it – that's what we meant.

Arteles, Finland, October 2021

Forty One

Though we would like to think that we pursue

A happiness that asks for nothing,

The old lie resides in the word 'renew'

Where deceit can be seen in their strutting.

A glittering reset remakes the man

Who baulked at the dark of winter's glory;

Frayed threads over a leviathan

Replaced by cashmere suits and history.

These giants of power are so well dressed

As they preach new ways to begin,

When they can only repackage much less

And neglect her sex, and some tones of skin.

      My forty-one years have not seen much change;

      A planet expires, a room's rearranged.

Reposal

Your face did not look like your own.
That day was my first in your home.

The tie you wore was maroon and white,
with a thin line of black.

We shuffled, queued and stood back,
the assembled sorries were off key

but music was never your thing, you
knew the whistle's pitch, its attendant silence.

Another world I adore but am not
cut out for, like this scene,

this awful tapestry you left us in,
siblings and cousins I only knew when

I stepped inside the bungalow
you grew up in. Your mother said my name,

sighed it, man, and said it was good to see me.
But how could that have been?

Your face did not look like your own.
That day was my last in your home.

The Scrap

Of course, we never spoke again –
Well, would you, after one like that?
I did see him once, at a distance,
walking down the middle of Shop Street
like Galway's very own tram
– indestructable and direct.

That was him all over, always,
and myself as well, once.
Youth, fury, and a brand new degree.
I still believe we were never wrong

until one of us thumped the other.

The Closest He Got To A Manifesto

There are so many birds – they are ceaseless.

I wish them well, weren't they here first?

The headlines, if you read them, are grim-grim –

Kill your phone – kill the radio.

If you can read from one end of the day

to the next, well, why wouldn't you?

Oh, the wild ways lead you outdoors – ignore

them today for James Ellroy or

Give Knaussgard a go; he's been waiting there.

Forget about your friends. Make new ones.

I'm serious: us humans thrive in print.

This is a day to go mental

about tomes, I mean lengthy ones, or poems

by Rita Ann, Sarah Clancy –

Make your list endless! Martina Evans,

Todd Swift. I could go on. I will!

Today is a sentence with no full stop

Like Mike McCormack's *Solar Bones*

or the much lesser known 'Notes From My Phone'

Have breakfast then read four chapters

At elevenish flick on the kettle

Talk to your ghosts, or sing too loud,

Have lunch at your leisure, love a dirty carb,

and then read for three more hours

Stick with the plot and you'll know what to say

when someone calls to talk at length.

The answer you'll have is the best one:

"I'm reading – yes – I'm reading now."

But But But

But I never sold oil, only bought it

But look where I live it's *so* cold!

But I did my bit, man, I protested

   and I cried when Kenny's was sold.

But I've always recycled, upcycled

   and look there's the tree that I sowed

But I always voted for Michael –

   well, sure didn't he fix the road?

But the world is for them that are growing,

   and won't they just learn to adapt?

How could we ruin it, without knowing?

   Oh! Please don't describe us like that!

I leave a future whose options are stark

You'll starve in the heat

or die in the dark.

Gone South

New Orleans,
the dream is in returning.
The South before me
as a dotted white line.
Solo this time around,
    but never alone.

New Orleans,
sing to me.
I'm sitting in Ahmed's taxi,
as he recites some Persian verse.
Later, in another cab,
the driver lauds her lover.
"I said to him 'boy, if I'd known
you were this good I'd have got with you
    years ago.'"

Louisiana, listen,
and follow me back.
To that June, with that girl,

and that washboard she bought
    to play Zydeco, baby.

Her thimbled thumbs were the din of those days,
but I no longer keen for her rickety-clack.

New Orleans,
louder please.
Call me back, ma belle ville.
Haunt these Galway days.

Remind me what it's like
to lament the heat,
the sweat on my skin.
Let me know how it feels
to be burning
from the inside,
out.

Those Hands

I.M. Ja Keane

Those hands

with a chopping board and knife

moving so quick you'd swear

they were being driven

by some demented anger.

But not all fury is destructive;

not every storm is sent to ruin.

Speed serves, especially here.

The art in a diced onion,

mere seconds dissected

- in a blink - by those hands.

Today, they are stilled

by something he could not see.

And now his name echoes

from the apex of the door,

from the beams of the ceiling,

and hers, too, longer gone

but louder for it.

The resonance of siblings
in an empty kitchen.

We all head towards that sound
though we won't know that it's there.

Terminal Point

Two cups, too much froth; you won't finish yours.

Galway, in Spring. Isn't it cold?

The waiter asks if we need more – jesus,

What to say to that? No, we're fine?

Just look at me here, the bachelor Lear,

You're regal, dressed for the legal

Cadence of our later days – clinical,

One could say. In the café, toast is

Burning – my nose is my saviour today.

'I'm late for work,' I say. 'I'll pay.'

The envelope is crisp as it passes

From my hand, to yours. Done. No more.

The Comedian

Take
Every time
I've laughed at him – I would lose count.
Less so these days because
he loves psychoanalysis,

But
That's the show.
I saw him improvise once in Galway
for forty-five minutes.
He talked about debt, how did he get

To
the point
where he owed millions to mad men
who threw cash out like it
was meaningless, and asked my friend

Why
borrow five

million, when we'll gladly give you ten?
A similar sum was
set before the comedian.

He
did not make
light of it, but what he said in the
King's Head made something more
from the black and the red, from

The
debit and
credit that went up noses in
the era of poses,
of Bertie and dig-outs and pricks

Who
backed horses
whose legs, being mortal, could not
withstand such a vampiric burden.
But we've moved on since, we're convinced

By

our noble

demeanour in a world we respect,

that we love and neglect,

that we'll leave to the hapless and

tell them :

"You're next."

Four City Stanzas

Dublin, I miss you. It's really that simple.
Gigs in the Bord Gáis, your fast talk.
Capel Street, you are beautiful, always
Buzzing – how you make me hungry!

I could devour that town's tarmacadam,
Then wander up to Camden Street
To talk in a bar to some randomer
And say I saw Arcade Fire

In a tiny dive before the fame came.
Then I'll shut up for the music.
It'll be Soda Blonde, Darragh O'Dea,
Ron Sexsmith, Liam O'Maonlaí

Or someone I'll see in the next Mojo
Which I'll buy in Galway, my first
Urban love, with its porous floors, its
Melodied weather and *Where's Wally* shore.

The Rage

The rage I would sooner forget.
Erase the evenings
      of infinite podcasts
      and the next thing
      you *really* had to watch.

The rage I would sooner forget.
Is it six yet?
      We all shout at the TV,
      don't we? When it's mute,
      possibly.

The rage I would sooner forget,
No more livestreams,
      because people on screens
      are aberrations,
      it's not music anymore –

it's an absence,

the lack of a seat
in the Town Hall
underneath me,

the lack of the lads,
my noisy army,
the lack of
a sympathetic engineer.

It's not music anymore
      it's just me imagining

which is not
      what the singing was for.

-   *Jimi McDonnell*
    16 / 12/ 2021

Bobby & James

Bobby and James running at speed
Music and words are all that you need

L.A. Noir and the Acid House scene
Twinned by the pulse of amphetamines

James got clean, but his head was still humming
The click of the pen drowned the internal drumming

Bobby tried everything, sang every style
He's still throwing shapes but his eyes are not wild

This pair craft a madness that rattles my skull
A Scottish-American hybrid that pulls

Me to pages whose rhythms are mute
'Til I write something brilliant, noble or cute

I'll wear myself down before I see myself right
I'll sing *Movin' On Up* at the end of the night

I've read *American Tabloid* three times in this life
But my lines are unfocused, my plot isn't tight

Though the verse that I'm feeling is not what I write
Their demented genius is my darkening light

Bobby and James running at speed
Music and words are all that you need

No Second Troy Deeney

after No Second Troy by W.B. Yeats

"...I don't like it when people with a status speak about politics. Do what you're good at doing."

- *Zlatan Ibrahimovic*

Why would I slate him 'cos he talks these days
So bitterly, or that he should of late
Have pined for eloquent men in silent days
Or scorned the so-so goals for the great,
Had he a crusade equal to his wages?
How could he be mellow with a mind
That Malmo forged as lethal as a fire
With a right foot that stole the show, a kind
Of hopeful limb for an age like this
Because   it   endures   and   can   still   earn?
What could he have done, being who he is?
Is there another Troy Deeney that he can shun?

Salthill

Salthill, the edge of Galway. I'm awake.
The city is a leaning tree, alive

In an ungodly gail, its roots brazen.
The town exhales, releasing car alarms,

The squawl of a horny cat, a weeping
Fence sings a sighing key and

In that breath, too – the ocean.
Galway's subconscious, salty and constant.

An ever-changing moving mass,
A hive for a swarm of swimmers,

A lush liquid that knows too well
The jagged caress of Clare.

From there the Burren looks over
At its wayward Connacht cousin

Who expands languidly, ever outward.
It makes Spiddal a suburb,

It eyes up Connemara and says
In a Galwegian purr, forgoing Gaeilge,

"You know you have the legs of a tidy town,
Those eyes glow like satellite cities."

But here Galway is spurned, rejected –
For how do you charm Cornamona,

Carraroe, Letterfrack, Lettergesh,
Tullycross, Roundstone or Renville?

You're wrong, Galway – jog on.
The rocks of Diamond Hill are

Impermeable to plámáis. They say

"Stay in your duplex, count roundabouts

Jeeps, and the dearth of cycle-lanes

Is mise an pointe is faide san Iarthar,

The western-most West, I cannot be
Subsumed by holiday homes

Class climbers or kindergartens.
Your expansion must stop! Take stock

And remember this : we only endure
When we co-exist."

The Cool Shade

She's two robins
Sham
She's the cool shade
      under a beech tree

She's chives in bloom,
Man
She's Salthill on Wednesday,
      when it's quiet

I'm two magpies, fightin' –
Lads, I'm drivin' myself spare again

But, in my time,
I've been a Studio One album
boomin'
in the kitchen

I've cooked for her
      and the taste was sublime.

You see, we've discarded humility
Or that might've been me,
Rantin again –
      and....

Here I come for the new lexicon,
The Humblebrag
The Guesstimates
and the Gooper Gomies
using LOL when they speak –
Sham!
I could rant all week

But she's two robbins,
She's the cool shade
      under a beech tree

Headford, May 2022

Acknowledgements

Thanks to Seán Breathnach, Aoife O'Kelly, Brian Cleary and Rory Dempsey for reading my work over the years and steering this book home. Thanks to the writing group which during its run included Trevor Conway, Jenny Hall, Aoibheann McCann, Conor Duncan and Sarah Clancy.

A massive thank you to everyone who contributed to the crowdfunding campaign for *After Them* – this book would simply not exist without you.

I also want to thank the MA in Writing from NUIG class of 2010, and dedicate this book to the memory of Davnet Heery – a force of nature and a true artist.

Some of these poems have previously appeared in *Crossways Literary Journal, Skylight 47* and *The Galway Review.*

I would like to thank Teemu, Francisca and Amber from the Arteles Creative Center in Finland. To the other writers I met there in October 2021 – keep writing, keep creating and keep adding logs to the sauna!

Printed in Great Britain
by Amazon